Confessions

Poems

Confessions

Abdenal Carvalho

Copyright ® Abdenal Carvalho 2020

Title: Confessions - Poems

Publication Date: 06/2020 - 1st Edition

Author review

Author's Cover Designer

Category: Fiction Romance / 115 pages

This work follows the rules of the New Spelling of the Portuguese Language. All rights reserved.

The storage and / or reproduction of any part of this work, by any means - tangible or intangible - without the written consent of the author, is prohibited. The violation of copyright is a crime established in law No. 9,610 / 98 and punished by article 184 of the Brazilian penal code.

SUMMARY

Start 9
- In love 11
- Sighs of Longing 12
- Small things 13
- My mistake 14
- It was so 15
- My regret 16
- Do not go away 17
- Farewell 18
- How Much Madness 19
- Loneliness 20
- Miserably In Love 21
- Tired of waiting 22
- Our Covenant of Love 23
- Confessions 24
- Need you 25
- It's hard to forget you 26
- Costumes 27
- Dreams 28
- Again 29
- Today 30
- Every morning 31
- Your Sweet Kiss 32
- I love you so much 33
- You went 34
- Decision 35

Nothing matters	36
Disappointment	37
Talking serious	38
Without you	39
Last words	40
A new restart	41
Besides me	42
Our Way of Loving	43
I need to tell you	44
How are you doing?	45
How to forget you?	46
On the other side of the Door	47
Can't Believe I Lost You	48
Everything Is Sad Without You	49
My Purpose	50
Today Early	51
The Flowers of the Garden of Our House	52
I learned to want you	53
Your look	54
After I met you	55
Like a fool	56
Forget me	57
Your Lies	58
Our Mistakes	59
I chose you	60
We were everything we could be	61
Nothing But You	62
The Peace of Your Smile	63
Routines	64
Love Rain	65
You went...	66

Folly	67
Tomorrow morning	68
Your kisses	69
A beautiful woman	70
Gentle Affection	71
Inside you	72
Every day	73
She Is Coming	74
Your Power	75
Burning Desire	76
Our Madness	77
The first time	78
Only you	79
The Sound of Your Voice	80
Do not go	81
Addicted To This Love	82
Love and hate	83
My thoughts	84
Who Am I in Your Life?	85
Help Me Forget You	86
Don't tell me goodbye	87
Your Pretended Way of Being	88
Between Four Walls	89
My life without you	90
After the Dream Is Over	91
Leave Me Here on the Floor	92
From heart to heart	93
I Was Everything For You	94
Wounded Soul	95
Tears	96
The Death of Our Love	97

Our Reasons 98

Under the Blankets 99

Can't Continue 100

I really love you.. 101

Allies In This Lov 102

To know you... 103

The rain falls.. 104

You Made Me Suffer 105

When You Want To Come Back 106

Good friends 107

Child's play 108

In this Great Absurd 109

Like a worm... 110

habit of loving you... 111

Our Love Game 112

Considerations 113

Start

In love

I loved you from the first time I saw you

I wished you so much that with such charm I almost went crazy

I wanted you more than anything, but out of shyness I remained silent, silent, desolate with such unrequited passion ...

My nights were cold, empty and meaningless

For years, lonely, I learned to talk in silence with loneliness

I confessed my pains to her, shared my illusions, sharing every depressing second, where my mind sometimes wanted to explode from thinking about you so much

It wasn't easy to resist so much nostalgia

Your goodbye created deep wounds inside me that still bleed my bitter heart to this day

I remain in love as before, my eyes still watch the horizon with hope in the certainty of seeing you return

However, the wind that breathed the perfume that enveloped your body was lost all over the world and never brought you back to me

I have nothing left, my pain is immense, I disbelieved in love and that's why I chose never to fall in love again.

Abdenal Carvalho

Sighs of Longing

I don't want to love you, feel you and wish

I don't want to remember the taste of your kisses, the warmth of your hugs, the illusion that made me believe in your false love

But it doesn't matter what I want

There's no use resisting

Because in the end I end up surrendering to this crazy passion again

Lost between one affection and another

Crazy to see you

You are my perdition

The madness that blinded my eyes and deceived my heart

The complete disgrace that came to destroy me

Made me fall to my knees at your feet, begging for compassion

He threw me on the floor and bleed my chest

I am a poor devil, completely humiliated, asking for a crumb of your attention

I am a lost, despised soul, thrown into the deepest precipice of your forgetfulness

Someone who can't forget you for a moment

A man who thinks of death all the time for not having you

Small things

A simple look

A word

A smile ... All of this can give rise to a feeling so deep that it will make our soul sigh

A kiss given with much love

An immensely strong hug

Promises made in the moonlight

Moments of intense pleasure ... Make it impossible to forget a past of immense happiness

Staying in front of the fireplace, admiring the burning of the wood

Our words spoken in a whisper

The kiss on the mouth, on the neck and all over the body

The taste of your mouth and your tongue screwing in one sex

Sliding into the most secret parts

Driving me crazy with lust ... That was etched in my thoughts forever

The farewell, your goodbye, the last time we were together in that soft, warm, cozy bed

The moment of your departure, the wave of your hands ... The day I died.

My mistake

I loved you like no man should have loved

I surrendered in full and without reservation

I let you dominate me, make me your slave

I abandoned my closest friends

I turned my back on them in exchange for your love

After a while I was forgotten, abandoned

The only thing left for me today is sadness and loneliness

I was wrong to believe your promises

I have sinned by believing it was important in your life

I was wrong to think that someone so selfish would be able to love

Now I just regret my desolation

I live this tremendous discontent

Looking at the void that surrounds me

Enjoying the pain that was planted inside the chest

Being obliged to accept the disrespect you had with me

In the dark of this room I find myself lost in so many thoughts

Mulling over my failure

Dying day after day for still wanting you

It was so...

We were everything a loving couple can be

We loved each other day and night, with each new minute we belonged to each other

I lost my mind and the strength to say no to all his pleas

I became addicted to you without knowing that under your wheel petals there were thorns

I gave you all my affection and for a long time I was lucky to be reciprocated

However, one day you didn't want me anymore and left reading my life together

It left me thrown to the dirty floor by the mud of loneliness and contempt

Since then I've been living like a shadow

I walk the streets that despite having so many people, walking from side to side, for me they are deserted

I'm similar to a cloud overhead and no one notices

A dry leaf that the wind blows at random, aimlessly, unnoticed

I'm a living dead, with no dreams or hope

Any useless, a single grain of sand among millions of others

A dark spot in the Universe, a dull star

Someone with no chance of being happy again

An unhappy person who ignorantly believed in love

My regret

I can't ask you not to leave, but I can beg you not to go now

Please stay a little longer with me, even if it's like friends, make this night our last night of love

Ever since you decided to leave the evil one of death you live close to me and I feel like giving up on life

This crazy longing that came to exist inside me is like an immense bonfire that burns my immensely bitter soul

Imagining to live without being able to feel the heat of your body again makes me crazy

Little by little I feel wasting away, breaking in my chest the hope of not losing you

Don't say goodbye, say you're kidding and you'll still be mine forever

My peace has come undone, everything seems to be lost, I can only regret

Do not go away

I will continue here, in this solitude, singing a sad song

The one we heard together for the first time when we met

When you taught me how to live and gave me so much affection

I remember our happy and dreamy past

Where we imagined living a future full of achievements and achievements

Now, when I need your warmth most, your hugs, I find myself alone

Don't use excuses to leave

Do not put obstacles to stay

You know your past doesn't interest me, I accept you anyway

Don't disappear, tell me where you are looking and I can't find

I go around, around street corners, bars of life and night parties

But I can't find you, it seems like you've been invisible or hiding from me

This old passion punishes my heart

I can't live anymore, I need to meet you again

Maybe the passion I learned to feel for you was the poison that made me go crazy

Maybe this is my fate, to die from loving you so much

So again I ask you, stay, don't leave me, don't go away

Farewell

Nothing can be sadder than goodbye

Nothing donates more than a farewell between people who love each other

Nothing is worse than being away from a great love

However, the most terrible thing is to lose those who made us happy

That sunny summer afternoon you're gone

Left me behind with tears in my eyes

I confess that I also cried, I couldn't contain so much emotion

The sun was hidden behind the water of that river where we often visit

And again I was there after your goodbye, now completely alone

I looked at the horizon, I saw the rays of daylight disappear

I felt as if the arrival of darkness was also saying goodbye to me

So I burst into sadness and remembered his departure

I wished to die in that moment so sad, so bitter

You're still everything to me, what I've always wanted, the best I've ever known

Goodbye, baby, I know you still love me, but you had to leave. adore you

How Much Madness

We were crazy, lost, wanton

Our bodies burned when they touched

The intense, deep kisses, full of burning desire

Nothing and nobody loved as we love

We deliver without reservation

We were not afraid of what might happen after each night together

Our bed was on fire, sheets were torn, our sexes looked like pleasure machines

But as everything in life passes, everything comes to an end, we get cold in the relationship, That desire to love you every day and every moment has died

Now, far from everything we were and felt, there was only a vague memory of how complete, happy, fulfilled we were

I wanted you so much and I know I was returned

Unfortunately time always takes care of changing things

Put everything in a new place

Rewrites a new story for each person

And we can't always stay in the same place

Stay in the same place and with the same people

So we can only move forward and hope that we can meet again

Why will this happen I will want to love you again, give all my love

Loneliness

She sat across from me, when I was staring at the blue wall of the room where I loved you so many times.

She laughed at my sadness, mocked the disgrace that fell on our house

And as an impotent being can tell you nothing

I found myself obliged to accept that affront

Swallow your disdain

She stayed there, clapping for my desolation

For the immense nostalgia I feel for you

For realizing that even after betrayed and cheated I still love you

Like a wretch the only thing I did was cry bitterly

Sick of passion for you, a thankless and compassionate woman

Yeah, I didn't even have the strength to react and try to forget you

The way was to admit my weakness, my lack of courage

Accept the fact that she was right to criticize me

To step on my head and call me slack

After all, it is not characteristic of a real man to go down that far

Accept such humiliation and continue to want you as I still want you

You are gone and only loneliness is left to see me suffer

Miserably In Love

The mornings are gone, the afternoon passes quickly, but the nights seem to last an eternity and insomnia haunts me because of the immensity of this longing that I feel for you

The clock hands on the wall froze or move

Time stopped after I was alone

It's winter and outside the rain falls incessantly

My mind is tired of remembering you so much

I'm slowly languishing, my emaciated body doesn't make any difference in the scale

I have lost hope that all this will come to an end

I stay locked up for days, I eat badly, my mouth doesn't want any food, even if my stomach complains about it

Death knocks at the door, I feel her breath in my ears, she holds my hand and announces my departure, but I'm not ready to give up waiting for her return yet

Baby, after I lost you I became a destroyed man, a lost soul, an unhappy, miserably in love with you

Tired of waiting

How long will I have to wait for your return?

I'm no longer strong enough to continue sitting in this chair

To remain lying in this bed

Tired of waiting for you

If you don't love me anymore and decided to never come back say it soon

Hurt my sad heart once and for all

Create wounds deeper than the ones I already have

Spill all the blood I have left

Be my executioner, my martyrdom, my desolation

Don't feel sorry for my pain

Don't have compassion for my anguish

After all, who has been the one who has always been a judge of me?

Who deceived me for so long?

Who played with my love?

Of course it was you who destroyed my peace

Who did so many bad things like no one else does

It was you who deceived me with false promises

That created false hopes

Made me love you blindly like an idiot, lose me in this crazy passion

Our Covenant of Love

-

We agree to forever love each other

Never give up on this love that changed our lives

That brought us together in a surprising way

Made us the happiest people in the world

We swore we would just live for each other forever

That nothing and no one would stop the realization of that dream

Our lives would be eternally linked regardless

But you didn't keep your promises and gave up on me

One day gone and never came back

That revolted me immensely

I was sick of missing you for a long time

Enough time to decide to forget you

However, how to forget a great love?

How to erase everything we live?

How can I stop wanting you like before?

How to live without having you by my side?

So I surrendered to the desperation to lose you, I suffered, I cried, I despaired all night and early morning without being able to feel your warmth

Confessions

I confess that I still love you

I still want you

That I can't live without you

I confess is madly in love with your way of being

For your charming smile

By the sound of your voice

For the taste of your kisses

For the beautiful way of listening

I confess that I'm crazy about the perfume of your body

By the tightness of your hugs

For your long hair

By the color of your eyes

For the dreams we dream together

I confess to be only yours and want you just for me

That life gets more colorful by your side

That I'm forever marked by this love

That nothing else matters, just make sure I have you every day

I confess not to consider my wishes

That I gave myself over to that passion, that I live to love you

Need you

Your absence mistreats my heart too much

Staying away from your kisses suffocates me

It makes me sad and life doesn't exist if I don't have you here

I need you like the earth and plants need the sun and rain

I need this love to live

To feel pleasure, joy, hope

I need your constant company

At all times realizing that I'm not alone

At all times I can hug you, kiss you, give myself

I need to daydream every day and when I wake up I can see you

Get lost in your charms

Go crazy under our sheets

I need to shout to the world that I found the woman of my dreams

I finally found the right address for happiness

That I'm the most accomplished man in this world

I need you all my life

Like honey bees

How my body needs health to live ... I need you

Abdenal Carvalho

It's hard to forget you

It's not being easy to erase you from the thought

I remember you all the time

Every second

All the time

It's hard to live like this

Always wanting to have you for me

Seeing you where I go

Feeling you in everything I do

Hearing you in the voices that speak

In the songs of birds

In the move of nature

It's hard to forget you

Because my eyes see you anywhere

Your shadow chases me wherever I walk

My paths always cross with yours

Even in the waters of rivers and seas I see the reflection of your face

Your look that admires me

Your smile that enchants me, hallucinates me

I can't forget you because deep down I don't want to get you out of your mind

Because to exist in this Universe without you is worse than death

Costumes

Nothing that we were in fact existed

Nothing we thought or said was real

Our love story was an illusion

Our dreams of happiness are silly

We were wrong for a long time

We pretend to be the impossible

We deceive ourselves and think we are happy

Today that everything ended, only the reflection of our ignorance remained

The marks of pain caused by the awakening of that sad reality

The shame of our thoughtless acts

So many betrayals, mistakes and lies

We were two pretended people

We wore masks like two clowns

Our life was a circus

You and I live for years in a ring

People believed what we invented

We did well as puppets of a false passion

We lie to ourselves and the whole world

It was all an arranged farce, invented

We are two cynics, two cowards and our history full of fantasies

Dreams

I dreamed of wanting you all my life

I dreamed of having you forever

I dreamed I would never lose you

I dreamed of your kisses

Your affection

Your charms

Your sweetness

I dreamed of never waking up from the dream of loving you

I dreamed of being yours everyday

I dreamed that you would be mine every night

I dreamed of the warmth of your body

Going crazy with pleasure

So much joy

I dreamed that our plans would come true

We would be a perfect couple

No lies, no empty promises

I dreamed of perfect love

I dreamed that nothing would be missing between us

I would give you the sky, I would give you the infinite

It would be your peace, your joy, your guarantee of happiness

Again

Again you left me saying nothing

Again I didn't know what to do

Your distance mistreats my life too much at all

I don't know if I can live without having you

Again my eyes got red from crying

Again I had to endure the pain of watching him go

Again I hurt my heart by leaving me

Again I woke up without being able to hug you

Again the sheets on our bed were empty

Cold without your presence

Useless without being able to warm you

Again I am here among these four walls to mourn

Lonely again

Again like a sucker who always forgives your mistakes

Again like a fool who gets madly in that false love

Again deceived, injured, betrayed, stabbed in the back and chest

Again aware that you don't deserve me

But unfortunately I can't get you out of my mind

Today

Today I woke up in anguish

Desperate for the lack of you

Today I will live another long day

The morning will be sad

The deserted afternoon

The night a hell face to face with loneliness

Today again I will look out the window hoping to see you return

Today again I will cry

Today I will admire the colorful flowers from the garden you planted

Today again I will feel the pain of your goodbye

Today I will not have peace

Today I'll be lonely again

Today my thoughts will be stuck on you

Today I will not notice the sunlight

Today I won't feel the cold rain

Today my existence will be a desert

Today the wounds on my chest will be open

Today I will be dead inside myself

Every morning

Every morning I think of you

Every morning I can't forget you

Every morning I wake up in love

Every morning I feel trapped in your love

Every morning I'm still yours

Every morning I realize I lost you

Every morning I see the distance that separates us

Every morning I miss you

Every morning I hear the birds sing

Every morning they remind me of your beauty

Every morning I admire nature

Every morning she asks me about you

Every morning i'm unhappy

Every morning it breaks my heart

Every morning my tears increase

Every morning nothing makes sense

Every morning I feel more and more forgotten

Every morning I find myself more and more deluded

Every morning I am dead inside, in total dismay

Your Sweet Kiss

Your sweet kiss poisoned me with passion

Bewitched my heart

Made me your slave

Chained me to your feet

Your sweet kiss blinded my eyes

I became dependent on you and your love

Caught me in the prison of your smell

In your taste chains

Through the webs of your way of loving

Behind the bars of your sex

Your kiss hallucinates me

Teach me to love you every day

More and more lost in this intense madness

Increasingly addicted to the delights of your body

Caught me in your clutches of seduction

In the mistakes of your affection

In the falsehood of your words

Your kisses make me sigh with longing

Your kisses dominate me, humiliate me, drive me crazy

I love you so much

It's too good to love you

It's too tasty so much pleasure

My life got used to your presence

I can't complete without your affection

Without your perfume, your smell, your woman's charms

I love you so much

I love you too much

I want you all day

Every second I miss you

The distance kills me

Torments my lonely soul

I love you like no other can love you

I wish you like no one will ever wish you

You are my everything

It's my delight, my best flavor

I seek you in everything that exists in this world

Because only in you I am satisfied

Only by your side I am happy

There is no yesterday or tomorrow, just the two of you and me

You went

You were the best of my dreams

The biggest mistake

What I liked the most

You were the most serious passion

The most sincere illusion

Everything else I thought to find

You were my best joke

The sweetest nonsense to make

The most delicious pain to feel

You were my greatest joy

Also my biggest disappointment

My biggest reason to live

You were my biggest nostalgia

The greatest happiness

The dream I intend to never forget

The most incredible adventure I lived

You were all happiness, all evil that did me good

And for all this I still feel you close to me again

Decision

I decided not to try to forget you

I decided to want and want you

I decided to do so many things without thinking

I decided to walk by your side even if sometimes you reject me

I decided that I won't lose you

I decided to hold you in my arms even if the distance tries to prevent

I decided that you will be mine

I decided to belong to you completely

I decided to unite our lives forever

I decided to never stay away from this love

I decided to tell you how much I love you

I decided to surrender to this passion without fear of suffering

I decided to face the illusion with more reality

I decided to pretend to have all the happiness

I decided to do everything to make it true

I decided to build a perfect world for both of us

I decided to be the owner of our destinations

I decided to govern our lives

I decided that nothing and nobody can separate us

Nothing matters

No matter your contempt

No matter your indifference

No matter your arrogance

No matter your pride

No matter your abandonment

Doesn't matter your goodbye

It doesn't matter to be too small in your eyes

It doesn't matter if you make fun of me

It doesn't matter if I step on your feet

No matter your insults

No matter your humiliations

It doesn't matter if you turn your back on me

It doesn't matter if my passion is your fun

No matter your criticism

It doesn't matter to be your doormat

A simple rug where you walk and tap dance

If you keep me on a tight leash

If you made me your slave

If you tie me to your want .... For me nothing matters if I have you

Disappointment

The disappointment of life leads me to death

Disappointment in friendships leads me to loneliness

The disappointments of the past and the present make me fear the future

Disillusionment in so many broken promises overwhelms me inside

Disappointment at being deluded suffocates me

Disappointment at seeing the truth in lies makes me pessimistic

Disillusionment in love keeps me from loving

I am disappointed by nature

I'm confused, scared, scared

I don't trust people, what they say, what they swear to do

Disappointment turned me into an undead

In a kind of ghost that only astonishes itself

In a close friend of solitude

Disappointment chases me wherever I go

She follows me everywhere

We are very connected

She mistreats me and I just cry

Disillusionment hurt my heart so many times that it dried up your feelings

Today it beats slowly, without force and without life

Disillusionment is like a poison that destroys the soul and our faith

Talking serious

Seriously, I don't even know the reason for these things

Seriously, I don't understand why I loved you

Because i wanted you

Because I chose to live so long with you

Seriously, I don't understand why we met

Why we sleep so many nights in the same bed

To unite our bodies and feel pleasure

Why I felt the least passion

Seriously, why are we in this conversation?

Why are you still crossing my path?

Why don't you say goodbye and forget what happened?

We are the opposite of each other

The reverse of what we could have been

The opposite of reason

The wound that won't heal

The blood that gushes nonstop

Seriously, get away from me, let's take opposite roads

Don't look back, because I don't want to be remembered

Seriously, I will never love you

Without you

Since our farewell the world has stopped

Since the last goodbye my sky has collapsed

My inner light turned to darkness

My feeling of happiness disappeared

I suddenly became speechless

Such sadness stole my words

Nothing is more terrible than so much longing

After so long awake

In the insomnia of a cold dawn

In desperation of not being able to see you

In the anguish of not being able to find you

I hug my pillow and imagine your warmth

Our moments of intense pleasure

It is terrible to wake up and realize that everything is over

I no longer have the strength to walk

I became a hostage to the slowness of my thoughts

Cause my mind just wants to remember what we were and what we did

My days are summed up in the inertia of our past

I'm bitter, hurt, hurt

Baby how hard it is to be without you

Last words

I say goodbye thanking you for letting me participate in your life

For tolerating my annoyances

For the many times I was stubborn and irritating

For talking so much and never listening to you

For discrediting your promises

For the ingratitude of not supporting their decisions

For refusing to accept your faults and defects

For the injustice of not making you happy

I say goodbye forever on this dark morning

Where even with the intense light of daylight

And despite the sun's rays warming us up

  We still feel cold

When certainty that everything is over is the only certainty that we have left

When we know that nothing we do will change this sad situation

When our eyes refuse to cross the same space

And the grudge took over the passion that we have felt for a long time

I'm leaving right now, when I wanted to stay

Hug you and start over from where we left off

Give us a chance and start over our beautiful love story

A new restart

Everything that exists today, existed yesterday and will be born again

So if everything that dies now can come back to life in the future

If we are the copy of the past now in the present

If tomorrow we write today

In the same way our love can resurrect

Rising from the grave of oblivion

Our thoughts will connect

Our hearts will love each other again

You and I will meet again to live an eternal passion

A new start is taking place now

A new hope has resurfaced

I can see our bodies glued together, full of desire

I will be your joy and you my peace

You will give me pleasure and I will give you happiness

You will never cry again with sadness

You will never again feel the pain of loneliness

Because I will live just to make you happy

Let's stop looking back, Let go of pessimism and the fear of surrender

We believe that everything will work out, because it is possible to start over

Besides me

Besides me, what do you have left?

Besides me, who will you love?

Besides me, who will make you be more loved?

Besides me, who will listen to you?

Besides me, who will understand you?

Besides me, who will know how to kiss your mouth?

Besides me, who will know how to give you pleasure?

Who will know how to undress your body with such affection?

Who will caress you with such madness?

Who will know where your weakest points are?

Who will touch your intimacy with such perfection?

Besides me, who will you be?

Besides me who will see you as a beautiful woman

Besides me who will value your kisses

Besides me, who will be excited by your moans?

Besides me, who will have a language that drives you crazy?

Besides me who will make you climb to the clouds

Who will make you cram on your bed, sofa, table and floor?

Who, besides me, will make you happy?

Our Way of Loving

We are equal in everything

We were born for each other

We know the exact moment to surrender

We know the right time to love each other

Nature admires and inspires us

The sun leaves us during the day

Night greets us at dusk

The waters of rivers, seas and oceans move serenely as they watch us pass

No other couple love each other so much

Nobody is astonished like us

Because we are second to none

Because we are soul mates

Because God created us

Our way of loving cannot be copied

Cannot be imitated or drawn

Me and you are perfection itself

The logical explanation of love and life

The very philosophy of human existence

Our way of loving will change the world

Abdenal Carvalho

I need to tell you

I need to tell you that I still love you

To say that life is sad and empty, when we are far away

That everything around looks gray

The darkness blinds my eyes

Sadness fills me with bitterness

That I'm nothing without you

I need to tell you that I was nothing before I met you

That nothing seemed to make sense

I lived to live

It was like a tree planted always in the same place

Little knew of the world

My gift is now dark

My future is uncertain

I don't feel like continuing

I need to tell you that in the loneliness I find myself I die little by little

I live crazy with nostalgia and it makes my heart sick

My pain is so great that I don't even see time go by

Whether it's day or night I don't even realize

I'm tormented by the fear of never seeing you again

For the anguish of losing you, of not having your love anymore

How are you doing?

How are you doing after our goodbye?

How are things after I left?

How is your dawn without me by your side?

How have you been without my presence?

Without my hugs?

Without my hot kisses that made you crazy?

How are you doing?

Tell me a little about your life

Tell me about your day and your evening

Tell me if you miss me, if you want to go back, if you're sorry

Don't be ashamed to speak, reveal all your secrets to me

How are you doing after that sad ending?

Is it good or bad in the new path you chose?

Are you happier with that other person or are you silent?

Did your heart really forget me?

Is there no trace of what we live in?

Do you sleep peacefully at dawn or do you think about us?

How are your feelings?

Don't you have a big wound on your chest inside?

Tell me now: How are you?

How to forget you?

How can we forget what we were all our lives?

How to forget what we say to each other in vows of love?

How to forget so many kisses?

How to forget our hugs?

How to forget your smile?

How to forget such passion?

How to erase your beauty from my mind?

How to just stop loving you?

How to wake up every morning without you?

How to smile in this despair?

How to sleep in this solitude?

How can I pretend to be happy if I am completely abandoned?

How to avoid so many tears?

How to forget about waking up alone in this bed?

How to forget you if I still love you?

How can you forget when I can still smell you?

How can you forget if I still smell your perfume?

How can you forget if you're part of me?

How to forget you if I live to love you?

How can I forget if what matters to me is you?

On the other side of the Door

Behind the door of life was our past

Behind the door hides so many memories

Behind the door we keep countless memories

Behind the door our story lives on

Behind the door there is still hope

Behind the door our dreams stand the test of time

Behind that door the longing calls us

Behind that door loneliness complains

Behind that door our passion insists on being felt

Behind that door there is still an empty bed

Behind that door is a room whose walls have seen us

Behind that door the sky blue painted in the four corners watched us

Behind the door many things remain as before

Behind the door nothing has changed

Behind the door, fate still writes the present and the future

Behind the door I'm still looking for you

Behind the door you still want me

Behind the door we are still immature

Behind the door we still love each other

On the other side of the door I still can't forget you

Abdenal Carvalho

Can't Believe I Lost You

No, I can't believe our love is over

That we parted without reason

That you said goodbye without any explanation

I won't be able to live without you

It won't be easy to forget you

Life without having you by my side will be an endless anguish

I won't be able to wake up every morning without seeing you

I won't be able to feed without loving you

I won't sleep through the lonely nights

I won't be able to leave the place without your hands to help me

The world will be too small in this dismay

The day will be dark

Colors will lose color

Nature will be silent

The birds will stop singing

The winds no longer blow your hair

The serene does not wet your body on moonlit nights

Your look no longer shines, nor does mine admire you

No, I can't believe I lost you

Everything Is Sad Without You

I need you all my life

I can't breathe or exist without you around

Everything in me needs to feel you, touch you

Nothing makes any sense if my eyes don't see you

One day comes and another goes

The nights come and then go

The hours go by suddenly that there is no time to think straight

The world seems to have gone mad

Everything is so different since you left

Even our house is no longer the same

The flowers in the garden of our house all died

I need this love just like the air I breathe

I miss everything good and beautiful that we live

My eyes look for you, but can't find you

My thoughts chase you in vain

I became a summer streak in this valley of tears

I stagger around the deserted streets

Played at negligence because of the disappointment of losing you

I'm a drop of water in an endless ocean

   I need to find you, because everything is sad without you

My Purpose

My purpose is always to love you

Never forget you

Is not to live without you

My purpose is to want you for life

It's never turning away from your love

Is to stay by your side

My purpose is to kiss you whole

Caress you the whole body

Kill you with pleasure every day

My purpose is to have you for me at dusk

And when I wake up I can still lose myself in your embraces

Go crazy in your charms

My purpose is to daydream in this sweet illusion

I give you my heart without fear

Believe in your love lies and in the fantasies of that happiness

Feel your hands in my hands

Your look in my eyes

My purpose is to want you for wanting until death do us part

Today Early

Today I thought about you

Today again I died of love

Today I felt my chest accelerate

Today I almost went crazy

Today I woke up feeling empty

Today nothing made sense to me

I didn't shower today

Today I didn't eat

Today don't even get out of bed

Today I got sick of myself

Today I was disgusted with everything

Today I wished it were yesterday

Today I wish it was tomorrow

Today it seems that never existed

Today is the worst day in the world

Today I feel filthy, completely insane

Today I woke up looking forward to seeing you

Today I couldn't forget you

This morning I returned to love you

Abdenal Carvalho

The Flowers of the Garden of Our House

Our house was so deserted after you left

The windows overlooking the orchard were blurred

They no longer allow me to see the nature we used to see

The doors closed and won't let me out

Getting through them became impossible

The walls of the room squeeze me

The sofa started to serve as a bed and pillows replace your arms

The cover no longer warms me during the cold of lonely nights

The light that was once so strong now reflects weakly on the blue walls that we painted together

The TV only shows nonsense and almost doesn't want to talk anymore

The music that plays only reminds me, so I keep it quiet

Silence takes over everything, it is silent everywhere

If it rains I hear the drops of water slowly falling on the roof

I feel wet for them, even when none of them can touch me

It dawns and the fog of the glass windows is broken by the heat of the sun

Soon I see the other side and what is still there

I'm sad to see what we plant together

I cry when I realize that the flowers in our home garden no longer exist

I learned to want you

I want you in my life

I want you for all eternity

I want you in my arms

I want you in every thought

I want you night and day

I want you to love you

I want you to kiss you

I want you for wanting you

I learned to wish you

I learned to look for you

I learned to dream about our love

I held to admire you

I learned to look in your eyes

I learned to miss you

I learned to feel your pain

I learned to feel your joy

I learned to feel your sadness

I learned to trust your promises

I learned not to fear your goodbye

I learned to believe in our happiness, I learned to want you

Your look

Your look fascinates me

This look of yours illuminates the densest darkness of my being

This look of yours calms me down

This look of yours fascinates me and teaches me where to walk

That look of yours tortures me

That look of yours is my madness

Your look makes me boy

That look doctrine me

That look hurts me and heals my wounds

That angelic look does me good

That look of intense shine makes me grow

That look makes me live

This look steadies my steps

This look guides me

This look shows me the way

Your gaze controls me

Your look makes me speechless

Your look shows me the future

Your look tells me that without you I don't know how to live

After I met you

After you everything changed

After you matured

After you learned to be myself

After you nothing was as before

After the first kiss

From the first hugs

From the first night of love

From the first pleasure

I never forgot you

You were my greatest experience

My greatest joy

My biggest sadness

My most intense way of living

My most unforgettable past

My most tense gift

My biggest adventure

If today I'm in love

If today I live to love

If today I believe in the impossible

Everything started to exist after I met you

Like a fool

I believed in love

I believed in Passion

I believed in true happiness

I believed in the sincerity of people

I trusted the truth

I trusted integrity

I trusted that it would be possible to love

I trusted that I could be loved

I shut up in the face of so many offenses

I was dumbfounded by those who confronted me

I didn't murmur in the worst moments

I forgave to be forgiven

I ignored it when I was despised

I said nothing to anyone who should listen

I was polite when mistreated

I smiled when I should cry

I sang in anguish, I danced in sadness

I rejoiced during the greatest despair

I reached out to those who didn't deserve it

Like a fool I loved you without being loved

Forget me

Don't remember my name

Don't remember my appearance

My perfume, my voice

Don't see me in your dreams

Don't feel me during loneliness

Avoid seeing me in your memories

Erase from memory what we live

Make me just a shadow of the past

I don't want to be part of your story

I don't want to be your memory

Don't think of me, Don't miss

Don't wait for me to come back

Don't keep looking back

Don't wait for me at the door

Don't look at me through the window

Don't consider me your friend

See me as the worst enemy

Don't get your hopes up

Do not Cry

Don't dream, don't have fantasies, just forget me

Your Lies

Everything we talked about

Everything we promise

Everything we once said

Nothing happened

Our words were vain

Our useless promises

Our empty ideas

Our dreams were lost in oblivion

Our voice was just a meaningless sound

Like the chime of any bell at the top of the tower

A song without lyrics

A poetry without verses or stanzas

An uninspired poet

  I said I loved you so many times

I heard you wanted me all the time

I imagined being loved

I loved you beyond what you deserved

I got lost in your mistakes

I learned to cry and regret your lies

Our Mistakes

How many promises have been made?

How many lies have been told?

How many illusions lived?

So many times I was wrong

So many times I've been disappointed

So many times I cried

Our life was full of fantasies

Falsehood surrounded us

Malice dominated us

Deception lay between us

Masks covered our faces

Our yellowish laughter disguised happiness

We live separately in the same house

We sleep under sheets poisoned by discord

We were just a fraud

I'm ashamed of everything we went

Damn illusion that held us for so long

We waste so much time pretending a love that never existed

We suffer in silence because we are afraid to admit our mistakes

I chose you

I chose you because I believed in your affection

I chose you because I wanted to be happy

I chose you because you were so beautiful

I chose you because I was blinded by passion

I chose you to be accepted

I chose you to brighten my chest

I chose you because your beauty was immense

I chose you because of your smile

I chose you because of your humility

I chose you for your loyalty

I wanted you to be just mine

I wanted you to share my feelings

I wanted you like never before I wanted someone

I wanted you because by your side I completed

I wanted you to expand my happiness

I wanted you to complete my life

I chose you to take the world by your side

I chose you to know the infinite

I chose you to touch the sky

I chose you because nothing is greater than our love

We were everything we could be

We were the truth

We were the lie

We were the charm

We were the biggest mistake

We were the joy

We were the most complete sadness

We did everything a little

And we ended up being nothing

We were the most, sincere reality

We were the most intense fantasy

We were perfect and imperfect

We were humble and proud

I was patient and irritating

We were the light and the darkness

We were good and evil

We were beautiful and ugly

We were big and small

We went the straw and the fire

We were the heat and the cold

We were passion and love we were everything we could be

Abdenal Carvalho

Nothing But You

Apart from you nothing exists

In addition to you what remains is sadness and loneliness

Beyond you what there is is an endless void

Beyond you life ends

Besides you the time to

Besides you my eyes don't see

I hear nothing but you

Besides you get lost on the way

Besides you there are thorns

Besides you there are many pains

Besides you there are many tears

Besides you day and night fall apart

Without you I look around and see nothing

Without you nothing desire

Without you my feet freeze

Without you I don't move

Without you my heart beats weak

Without you I shut up

Without you my mouth closes, Without you I say nothing

I at all failure, because there is nothing but you

The Peace of Your Smile

In your smile I find everything I need

In your smile I find joy

In your smile I complete

In your smile I realize

In your smile I am all and nothing at the same time

In your laughter I'm loved

In your laughter I fall in love

In your laughter I charm

In your laughter I calm down

In your laughter I shut up

In your laughter I feel your affection

In your laughter I feel your warmth

In your laughter I feel your love

In your smile I'm impressed

In your smile I fall asleep

In your smile I deserve you

In your smile I can die of pleasure

In your smile I can forever live

In your smile I can wake up happy every morning

It is not possible to exist without the peace of your smile

Abdenal Carvalho

Routines

Every day I wake up and see you again in my thoughts

I feel your presence wherever I go

If I'm at home I see you walking through every room

If I'm in the garden the scent of flowers reminds you

If I walk the streets of the city your image is reflected in the windows

You appear on every corner of the streets where I pass

Your face is drawn on the walls of skyscrapers

On billboards, your eyes can't get enough of following me

Even the winds that circulate through the avenues cry out your name loudly

Everything repeats

Everything happens again

You insist on staying in my mind

I hear your voice

I hear your walk

I smell your perfume in my nostrils

I remember your girlishness

Your husky voice

My mania to provoke you

To drive you crazy, Your woman spell

This pertinent craze for wanting you, this endless routine of passion

Love Rain

We loved winter

We played under the rain that fell and wet our bodies

I thought it was beautiful to see your dance under the drops of water

The movement of your long hair

The waltz we danced with

We were two teenagers in love

Completely unrelated to time

We gave little importance to tomorrow

Our dreams were summed up in the love we felt

In the passion we lived with each new day

I loved you more than anything

You also wanted me beyond your strength

Nothing could be more perfect

We were able to live a complete feeling

Without any spot of infidelity

No fantasies or malice

For this reason, I miss this immensely

So whenever it rains again I remember you

So I wanted to repeat our history, those beautiful rains of love

You went...

My greatest perfection

The biggest attraction

The greatest feeling

The biggest thought

The most complete joy for my heart

The naughty smile

The joy in sadness

Who made me be a boy again

That strengthened me in uncertainty

It was the most complete certainty

The most sincere passion

The most intense pleasure

The fire that set my body on fire

That threw flames on my bed

Who day and night cherished me

Who hugged me strongly during the cold nights

You were what this world doesn't exist

You were what not even the Universe knows

You are my infinite longing, it's all for me

Folly

Your folly doesn't let you see that I love you

Your folly does not allow me to understand my reasons

Your foolishness makes you insensitive

Your folly hardens your heart

Your folly despises me

Your folly hurts me, treads me, throws me down

Your stupidity does not let you realize my enormous passion

Your stupidity blinds your eyes

Your stupidity prevents you from realizing the affection I give you

Your stupidity separates us

Your stupidity puts an end to everything

Your stupidity destroys what I feel for you

Your folly has put us so far away

Your stupidity created this discord

Created this hurt

It created this indifference

It created so much pain

Created huge wounds

Left us with no way out

It was your stupidity that made you lose me through foolishness

Abdenal Carvalho

Tomorrow morning

I intend to wake up and no longer remember you

I am willing to forever forget you

I intend to smile again for life

I want to wipe away my tears

I want to jump for joy

Being able to hug me

Kiss me

Make me happy

Tomorrow will be a new start

I will have everything I deserve from myself

I won't let others tell me who I am

Nor what should I do

Where to go

Who to talk to

Choose my friendships

Night passes and dawn approaches

The darkness still remains on the sides and above

But soon the sun will rise, the light will reign

Nothing and no one will stop me from changing my story

Because I already decided that everything will be renewed for me tomorrow morning

Your kisses

They leave me suspended from the earth

Give me wings to fly

Feed my soul

Strengthen my hope of being happy

Speed up my heart

Increase the passion I feel for you

Are my reason for living

Are my joy

Are my happiness

Your kisses make me dream

Make me wish I was always by your side

They hold me to your way of being

They enslave me in your love

In them daydreaming

I feel loved

I am completely in love

Go crazy with pleasure

I learn to want you

For them I do not forget a single moment

A beautiful woman

I fell in love the first time I saw you

I went crazy with the desire to own you

I screamed loudly in my heart that I wanted to be yours

I wanted to kiss your mouth

Then go down your entire body

I got so horny

An inexplicable madness came over me

You were so beautiful

Perfect in all things

Your eyes bewitched me

Your smile held me so beautiful

Your voice was like the whistle of the winds

The scent of flowers

The gentle fall of rain

The serene of dawns

You were synonymous with purity

The certified copy of divine perfection

The light of the most beautiful moonlight

The sun's rays in an intense summer

The singing of birds at the dawn of each new day

Gentle Affection

I fell in love with the softness of your kisses

I fell in love with the softness of your hugs

I fell in love with the delicate way of speaking

I fell in love with the sensual way of your walk

I loved you for the softness of saying "I love you"

I loved you because you loved me first

I loved you because you gave yourself up

I loved you because it would be impossible not to love you

I gave myself up because you knew how to conquer me

I surrendered because you knew how to accept me

I gave myself up because I wasn't afraid to donate my heart

I gave myself for your sincerity

I gave myself up because I saw no evil in you

I gave myself up because I received love without falsehood

I want you in my life forever

I want you permanently

I want you till the end

I want you even after death

And if I'm lucky, I will continue to feel that gentle affection in the hereafter

Inside you

I want to dwell in your heart

I want to be in your thoughts

I want to be part of your memories

Navigate your blood

  I want to live in your cells

Float in your imagination

Be the light of your eyes

The charm of your smile

The warmth of your hugs

The taste of your mouth

The sweet of your kisses

I want to be the shower water

The soap that slides over your entire body

The towel that wipes you

The clothes you wear

The shoe that puts you

Every strand of your hair

The delicacy of your hands

The softness of your skin, Your charming expression

  Your welcoming way, I want to be everything, I want to be inside you

Every day

I remember you all the time

I can't get you out of my mind

See you in my dreams

I feel you in my bed and up

I see you by my side every moment

When I'm walking. When tiredness forces me to sit

When I need to breathe

When I close my eyes

When admiring the stars

When I look at infinity

When I'm happy or upset

If I'm at lunch or dinner

If I'm in the bath, in bed, or anywhere in the house

If reading a book

If painting a picture

Whether I imagine something old or new

Whether crying or smiling

If I hear a beautiful melody

If I'm singing a beautiful song When I talk to someone

If I speak with loneliness, in the present or in the hereafter, you are with me every day

She Is Coming

I know my great love exists

I know she's somewhere

That one day we will meet

Let's finally meet

Our hearts are desired

We were born for each other

We are soul mates

Nothing will stop our meeting

Because fate wants it that way

So God wrote our story

She certainly looks for me

I am undoubtedly looking for you too

I want to hug you with immense tenderness

Feel the taste of your kisses

Your body heat

Going crazy with happiness

Always sleep and wake up beside you

Numb with pleasure

Love her for all eternity

I am very happy because she is about to arrive

Your Power

You have the gift of conquering me

The gift of deceiving me

The ability to seduce me

You have the strength that dominates me

The wisdom that teaches me to want you

The mystery that makes me go crazy

You have my soul in your hands

My heart thrown at your feet

My life completely enslaved in that love

You are the most important to me

You are the air I breathe

The water that quenches my thirst

The day sun that illuminates me

The darkness of the night that throws me into solitude

You are my infinite joy

The most terrible sadness

My best salvation and worst condemnation

You are my everything, my nothing, I surrender to your power

Burning Desire

I possessed you with such desire that I took you to the clouds

I penetrated to the center of your pleasure

I invaded your body with mad fury

Like a wild animal made you moan and rave

My savagery made you roll your eyes in a deep faint

I turned your body inside out

I was terribly mischievous

Naughty, ruthless, but incomparably good to feel

I made you crazy, I made you tremble all over

My wickedness did you good

It left you disheveled, excited, burning with lust

I woke up the wanton woman in you

I made you cry, smile, sing, dream

I gave you reasons to exist

I gave you all of me

I filled you with what was missing

I filled your life I completed your world

I was your past, present and future

I was your truth, your lie, reality and fantasy

I was the awakening of your greatest illusion

Today I am your happiness, your peace, your most ardent desire

Our Madness

Like two crazies we've been carrying our whole lives

We feared nothing and did not respect anyone

We were crazy, untamed, rebellious by nature

We didn't listen to our parents or older people

Advice had no effect on us nor did it hold our feet

We follow the outside world ready for our follies

We seemed to be dominated by evil

Darkness enveloped us and the light rejected us

I was a son of evil and you were a daughter of perversion

We took pleasure in sin

We were pleased with our crazy

We felt fulfilled with our childish attitudes

But time passed and we grew up

We mature for life

Our concepts have changed

The time for responsibility has come

True love has charged us for all mistakes

We understand that nothing in this world is how we think

So we stopped. We split up

We said goodbye and our follies ended

Abdenal Carvalho

The first time

Everything was transformed, everything was made

When we met and learned to love ourselves

It all happened so suddenly that our minds got stuck

Our bodies wanted each other

There began our great passion

Our friends soon realized that something special would happen

They supported us and did not for a second try to separate our worlds

Joy adorned our lips

Such a strong union held our passionate hearts

Some didn't even believe that we could want each other

However, we were truly happy

There was no space for sadness between us

We were never alone, because they kept each other company

However, nothing is perfect

Nothing exists without finding its end

So that great love also ended

Our hands came loose, our breasts beat weaker

We died little by little, disillusionment came and the brightness faded

We were really happy, we were incomparable from the first time

Only you

Only you understand me

Only you understand me

Only you know how I feel

Only you know me so well

Only you listen carefully to my voice

Only in your arms can I be happy

Just by your side I feel fulfilled

Just when we're together I complete

Only the two of us are so alike

Only your words clearly tell me what to do

Only your smile soothes me

Only in you comfort me

Only your body warms me

Only in it do I kill the cold of loneliness that invades my soul

I want you so much

I need you so much

I look for you everywhere

I want to find you at any cost, in any corner

In this world nothing else is of value to me, only you

Abdenal Carvalho

The Sound of Your Voice

Calms me, Cheers me up

It makes me feel joy to live

Cure me all diseases

Make me sleep. Make me grow

Fills me with hopes

Make me go back to being a child

Turns me into a new man

Show me the way to walk

Wipe away the tears

Guide me through the hands towards the unknown

Feed me with immense happiness

It gives me contentment

Increases the brightness of my eyes

Makes me sure to be happy

Strengthen my hopes

It brings us closer and closer

Makes us more passionate

Helps us to cross obstacles

It makes me float in this love

Make me daydream, nothing tastes better than hearing the sound of your voice

Do not go

Don't go to this adventure life

Don't go to a new misfortune

Don't go, don't leave me, be calm and everything can improve

Don't go astray

Don't go looking for a new love

Don't go without hope

Don't go like a child who on a whim will suffer

Don't go into a future without any certainty of happiness

Don't just believe me your uncertain dreams

Don't go empty-handed

Don't go without guarantees

Don't go foolish

Don't go towards the unknown

Don't go so alone

Don't go with so many hurts

Don't go on that thorny path

Don't go without my protection

Don't be silly

Don't be childish ... Don't go

Abdenal Carvalho

Addicted To This Love

You are my daily addiction

What I miss most

Sometimes I even forget about myself

But I don't forget this love

I can't stop thinking for a minute

It's like it's my food

The air I breathe

The biggest reason for my existence

When I'm by your side time goes by and I don't even realize

When we are together the hands of the old clock on the wall freeze

It's like nothing else exists but you

Wanting you makes me so good

It leaves no room for sadness and loneliness is forced to move

I'm addicted to your kisses

In your hugs

In your pleasure

In your way of being

To speak To act

To surrender ... I'm addicted to this love

Love and hate

Sometimes I don't understand my heart

There are times he wants you

There are others who hate you

If in a second he longs to find you in another he prefers never to see you again

If at a given moment in life he seeks your presence

Hours later despises you

This situation drives me crazy

It makes me completely confused

That makes me mute, isolated, I avoid talking to other people

I am a strange man, of few words and lonely

My neighbors seem to hate me

They even seem to be afraid of me

Some laugh at my misfortune, if they could they would throw stones

I have the appearance of a weakling

I behave like crazy

But what can I do to change this condition

Is there a huge confusion in my being?

For you I got lost inside myself

For you I entered this maze

For you I became love and hate

My thoughts

I can't think of anything but you

I can't think about tomorrow because it doesn't exist

I don't want to stick to the past because it's already broken

I can't imagine what the next minute will be like, because I don't even know if I'll be alive

My mind is blank

I erased all my history lived by your side

Lived with family and friends

I don't remember who I was or want to know what I am or will become

I'm like a tree planted in the same place for years

I'm like the bird that always sings the same song

The hands of an old clock that always mark the same hours

The east wind that repeatedly blows the four corners of the earth

The rain in winter, The sun in summer

Day and night

All these routine things that never change

That repeat throughout the year and continue the same way

Doing the same things, Existing just for existing

So I chose to stay here

Silent, without speech, without sound, without flying in my thoughts

Who Am I in Your Life?

Maybe I'm the best of your life

Maybe it's your biggest event

Who knows I may be your happiness

Or don't go beyond the biggest disappointment

I can be your peace

I can be your joy

I can be everything you most desired

Maybe I can be your best friend

Your greatest passion

Your anxiety

Your most complete certainty

Your most complex hope

Your water, your thirst, your wine, what feeds you

I would like to be your everything and your nothing

Your most delicate smile

Your tightest hug

Your most distant look

Your most charming dream

Your purest love

Your most sensitive, most loving side ... After all, who am I in your life?

Help Me Forget You

I don't want to feel you anymore

I can't bear to remember you anymore

I no longer intend to be stuck with you

I can no longer have peace by your side

So get out of my life

Set my heart free

Release my hands once and for all

Forget that one day we love each other

That we were happy

That we complete

Go along with the first wind that passes

No need to go back or send messages

I don't care how your day is

If your nights are happy or lonely

If you think of me or if I became a vague memory

I want to be a dusty book on your shelf

Whose pages remain intact for so many years

Aged by time and without a word

I just want you to go away and help me forget you

Don't tell me goodbye

Hey, it's outside, it's dawn. It's time for you to leave

The morning is so beautiful, came to say goodbye

The trees dance in the wind

The sun hides behind the hill, is still waking up

Their bags remain on the sofa in the living room where we often stay

Where during that last night we love each other

We roll over the flowery carpet we got when we got married

We cried together at the farewell that would happen early

And now it's time to say goodbye

On the coffee table several empty bottles

We drink our favorite wine and eat the favorite snack

It was moments full of homesickness even though we were still here

In the same house where we lived for several years

Where countless times we swear eternal union

Where we smile because of our own jokes

We mourn our failures

We find the strength for new beginnings

We dream without fear of ever achieving ideals

We wake up every day with the certainty that our love was forever

Now to learn to forget you, but I ask you not to say goodbye

Abdenal Carvalho

Your Pretended Way of Being

I was wrong with your sweet smile

With your beautiful voice

With your look like a girl in love

I mistook your mistakes for true passion

Ages as the most beautiful part of nature

Like the blue of the sea

The colorful of the flowers

The colors of the rainbow

I stuck in your charms

I let myself be chained to your kisses

I was blinded by your exponent appearance

Fall to your knees in your presence

The rays of your radiance froze me

I was overwhelmed, grounded in this crazy passion

My days without you were empty, colorless, in black and white

I became nobody if I couldn't see you

If I couldn't touch you

If I looked around and wasn't close to me

I suffered a lot, I almost died because of your pretended way of being

Between Four Walls

There we surrender ourselves

There we lost ourselves in that intense passion

There our sheets were set on fire with so much desire

There we were two flaming firebrands

There we were like live embers among the flames

We were astonished by those who saw us

We were the envy of those who could not live so crazy

We were everything we wanted to be

You and I have become the symbol of debauchery

We use our bodies in bondage to the most terrible sin

I owned you like a wild animal

You behaved like prey that quenched my hunger for sex

How many things we invent

How much immorality we did

We laugh at our own folly

We didn't respect the holy or the sacred

Everything for us was allowed

What happened there was cause for laughter after

We were immensely happy

We live immensely crazy things within those four walls

Abdenal Carvalho

My life without you

Without you I do not know how to live

Without you the loneliness is great

Without you there is no hope

Without you the longing is immense

Without you I despair

Without you life doesn't make sense

Without you the nights become empty

Without you the light turns to darkness

Without you my pain further increases

Without you nothing exists

Without you I give up everything

Without you mornings don't shine

Without you the afternoons are monotonous

Without you nature is sad

Without you there is no pleasure

Without you insomnia chases me

Without you I'm so sad. Without you death surrounds me

Without you I get lost in infinity

Without you my cry is huge. Without you I feel lost

Everything falls apart, everything is lost, everything is empty without you

After the Dream Is Over

I learned to have you with me every day

I learned to wake up next to you

I learned to feel you

I learned to touch you

I learned to remember how much we loved each other

I learned to want you

I learned to be your greatest passion

I learned to be loved

I learned to hug you with all the strength of my arms

I learned to give myself to your love

Today I had to change my way of being

Today I had to stop loving you

Stop wanting you

Forget your hugs

Erase your image from my mind

Don't feel the taste of your kisses anymore

Waking up without you by my side

Not being loved anymore

Can't touch you. Learning to exist in that solitude

I had to know how to lose you after the dream is over

Abdenal Carvalho

Leave Me Here on the Floor

Since the day you left I couldn't live anymore

After your goodbye nothing left

My gaze that once had a strong glow went into complete darkness

My smile was so cheerful it turned yellow

If before I was happy I became an abandoned man

Being without you is too painful

There's a wound inside me that burns endlessly

Even my shadow doesn't follow me anymore

It has become difficult to walk and I stand still without moving

His absence is an immense sacrifice

I miss you wherever you are

My chest throbs fast

I feel my blood running through my veins at high speed

I lack the air and it becomes difficult to breathe

I became drunk

The strong drink my greatest companion

Addiction enslaves me

My head is numb daily

I can no longer be conscious. Without you I am completely taken by the revolt

I would like to ask you to come back, but if not for love leave me here on the floor

From heart to heart

Stay here closer to me

Listen to everything I want to tell you

Come closer and listen to my voice

Let me tell you what I have inside my chest

I tried to forget you but there's no way

The more I try to get you out of my head the more I remember you

The more I try to erase from memory the more I remember our love

Sometimes I torture myself for the guilt of losing you

Sometimes I believe it was just me who made a mistake

But something screams out loud that I need to forgive myself

That I need to move on

That I must accept my mistake and start over

Come over here and tell me if I'm still part of your memories

If I'm still present in your thoughts

If somehow I'm still alive in your life

If somehow you still haven't forgotten me

Come, sit here, let's talk like two adults

Stop avoiding me, let's be honest

  Let us speak only the truth from heart to heart

Abdenal Carvalho

I Was Everything For You

I was everything a woman could want

I was your day, the morning and the sunset

I was the pleasure that made you crazy

I was the dream that came true

I was your greatest truth and the bitter lie

I was your most complete pleasure that shook you

I was your moments of peace

I was your cry and your joy

I was your song in the happiest hours

I was your tears in the minutes of despair

I was what you weren't looking for

I was the most interesting thing you wanted to find

I was the best

I was the worst

I was your summer and winter

I was your spring without the scent of flowers

I was the birds singing at sunrise each morning

I was your color when sadness left your existence black and white

I was your flower garden, your most beautiful landscape

I went to you everything that a great love owes and can be

Wounded Soul

Love you was a mistake

It was a tremendous mistake to love you

I wanted you madly

Like a madman I wished you night and day

If today I cry it's because I deserved it

If today I suffer it is because I tried

If today I regret it is because I insisted

There are things in life that we should avoid

And I should have avoided falling in love

You are an adventurous woman

Don't know gives value to a great love

It's the kind that doesn't mind hurting or hurting

It is insensitive and vulgar

Behind so much beauty lies the root of deception

The bitter root of pretense

Lie is your main brand

Your heart is filled with evil

I was a complete idiot to surrender to that passion

Because of my naivete today I have my soul wounded

Tears

Part of me still wants you

Part of me wants you

Part of me seeks you

Part of me whispers your name

But my heart rejects you

My body feels repulsion

My thoughts forget you

My eyes despise you

In my world there is no place for you anymore

You are a memory I intend never to remember

I suffered for you

I cried for you

For you with deep wounds I bled

I was ashamed for you

You do not deserve me

You are the most despicable being I know

You no longer exist for me. I will resist your false love for life

For you I will never shed my tears

The Death of Our Love

Yesterday I went to the cemetery

Yesterday I was present among those who wept

Yesterday I saw a coffin going down to the grave

Yesterday I witnessed a funeral

Yesterday I watched the burial of the one who united us for so long

At that sad moment the wind stopped blowing

The trees no longer danced under their packs

Our hair didn't receive its caresses

We didn't even hear your whistle

Death also appeared there

She reigned all over the place

An air of sadness spread over everything and everyone

Something dark made our skin crawl

It was the moment of farewell

When the end of everything we live has come

The prepared deceased succumbed

The land on it was cast

Gradually we saw for the last time who joined our hands

The one who made us lovers

That morning we watched the death of our love

Our Reasons

I blame you for the end of our love

I hold you responsible for our fights

For the countless disagreements

By indifference

For the silence that silenced our voice

That prevented us from saying what we felt

That so many times made you put up with insults

I blame you for the guilt felt

For the deep wounds

For the evil we did together

I blame myself for blaming myself

For accepting your mistakes

For not saying in time what made me feel

I blame myself for the cowardice of loving you despite everything

I blame myself for not reacting

For waiting for time to put everything in place

For crossing his arms, when he should take a position

I blame myself for all things

For all our defects

I blame myself for not understanding our reasons

Under the Blankets

There we loved each other until we felt our bodies faint

There we would surrender until our strength ran out

There I was your wildest animal

There you were the most ferocious woman I ever met

There I was completely yours and you totally mine

There we get lost in the time of love and passion

The satin sheets kept us warm in winter

They witnessed our follies

We did a little of everything

Did you know how to drive me crazy

And I learned you more and more to drive you crazy with pleasure

Between four walls I took you to the clouds and you made me see the sky

There seemed to be a little piece of paradise

Maybe that's why I miss it so much

That's why I miss you so much

That immense happiness came to an end

The dream is over and there is only the memory of what we were and lived

Now I just imagine missing so many good things that we live

I remember our history lived under the blankets

Can't Continue

How can I move on?

How can I be myself?

How to survive so alone?

How to look to the future?

How to dream without certainty that you will return?

How to believe in tomorrow in this loneliness?

How to be happy

How to wait for your return?

How to avoid such revolt?

How to have any hope?

How to be patient?

How to have peace?

How not to suffer? How not to cry?

How to walk without holding your hands?

How to get up when falling?

How can we not stumble over so many disappointments?

How can I stand firm if my strengths are gone?

How to breathe without smelling your perfume?

How do I sleep and wake up when I'm dead without you?

How can I stay alive if I can't go on?

I really love you

Don't be fooled by false promises

Many will come and say they love you

But it will all be an illusion

My heart belongs to you and my life is entirely yours

Don't get carried away by those who just want your body

Who only want to experience the taste of your kisses

Knowing your intimacy

Discover your nudity and then spread rumors

We belong

The Creator united us with a strong bond of love

Don't listen to lies

Don't lean your ears to empty proposals

Be mine entirely

Enjoy our nights together like it's the last time

Use your wisdom to separate what is real from illusions

Make use of your intelligence not to be deceived

Let yourself be loved by whoever wants you forever

Look at me and see a man totally in love

Only I can give you what you are looking for

Only with me will you be happy because I really love you

Allies In This Love

We are connected in the same feeling

In the same thought

In the same reason to live

We are only one heart

One ideal, one dream

One wish

You exist for me and I for you

Our souls are trapped in each other

We are the same light, the same brightness, the same reflection

We are the water of the oceans, rivers and the sea

We are the nectar of flowers

The honey sweet

Flying bees

We are the dance of the trees

The blowing of the winds

The rains fall

The light of the sun

We are accomplices, allies in this love

To know you

It was all so fast

Without any promise I accepted you in my life

I was in a hurry to win your heart

I was afraid that someone else would take my place

So I wasted no time and held your hand

We went out somewhere and there I confessed you are in love

I was not ashamed to say what I felt

That day I gave myself totally to you

And even today I don't even think about losing you

In no other moment have I been so happy

My joy was meeting you

We are an almost perfect couple

There is a sincere complicity between us

Few love each other as we love each other

Almost no one respects himself so much

If it could be a bird my song would be just to praise you

Magnify you before nature, the world and the infinite

If I could I would give you the sky, baby

If it were mine all the power would put you above the stars

Because nothing could be more wonderful than meeting you

Abdenal Carvalho

The rain falls

It rains outside and it's so cold in here

As I die of longing and my heart cries out your name

He calls you, calls you, calls you

Water droplets hit the roof hard

Everything around is wet

Plants are washed by the rain while animals hide

They seek shelter, flee the storm

Just as I try to run away from loneliness and longing

The picture on the wall holds your portrait

The image aged by time seems to have life

Ali you still smile at me

Your eyes never stop seeing me

It really seems to be here

Tired of being in the living room, I climb the stairs

I go to the room where we slept together one day

I can't lie on that bed and choose the tiled floor

But there you also walked and it becomes impossible to forget you

Everything reminds us both, it has your smell, your flavor

These things remind us of our love as the rain falls

You Made Me Suffer

For you I cried whole nights

I bittered for you

I mourned for you

I despaired for you

I almost died for you

I didn't eat for you, I lost weight

I lost sleep for you

For you I slept several nights

For you my life was worth nothing

I missed you so much

For you despair has taken over me

I suffered a lot for you

For you I wished death

For you everything ceased to exist

I lost happiness for you

I lived halfway through you

For you nothing was more like before

For you nothing else had the same value

Cause you made me suffer

Abdenal Carvalho

When You Want To Come Back

The door of my heart will be closed

In it nothing is as it was before

He lost confidence

Don't want to love you anymore

No longer want to suffer for this love

In his absence he suffered a lot

On your return he will despise you

Because he still has a minimum of pride of his own

And will be able to reject your false affection

Your false words

Your promises full of mistakes

My heart loved you madly

He desperately wanted you

But for your contempt you forgot

Almost died for so long waiting for your return

However, time healed his wounds

Healed your pain

He has now found true happiness

There is no more mark of your evil in it

So remember all of this when you want laps

Good friends

From lovers we were, we became just two acquaintances

Wounded by time and so many sad things that we live

Of two lovers we ended up as strangers on the same road

Nothing could be better after so much suffering

Today I see you as any person

You don't seem to even notice my existence

The passion that we once felt turned into hatred and bitterness

The old love we live died on the way

Our given and received affections become thorns

That are so sharp they pierce our flesh and torment our minds

The unhappiness was tremendous to the point of suffocating

The sadness was so great that it almost killed us

What's left of what we were?

What is the result of what we plant?

Maybe just two wounded hearts

Who knows, we may still become good friends.

Child's play

We were really fun

We were great friends

We did everything in complete innocence

Nothing was seen as absurd

Our bodies embraced without malice

We touched, we kissed in the simplicity of boys

Your hands in my hands

Your mouth in my mouth

Your sex in my sex

Our hidden desires

Our hidden desires

But the time came and everything took

Erased what was beautiful

Undo what was perfect

And from imperfection we were taken

By the harsh reality awakened

With the arrival of maturity we wake up

And we realized that from then on everything was a sin

Our actions would have serious consequences, it was no longer a simple child's play

In this Great Absurd

But what a tremendous thing to lose you

What a huge loss to live without you

And now what do I do to continue in this darkness

For you were the brightness of my life

You were the reason for everything I became

The energy that strengthened me

That kept me going

Immense injustice made me destiny

It put me in the most terrible contempt

I got stuck in the webs of loneliness

I can't get rid of the chains of suffering

My thought doesn't rest from reminding you all the time

I was in this torment that massages my heart

A soul lost in the darkness of longing

Dying inside like a tree that dries and bears no fruit

Damn those who like me live

Because they feel the same pain that burns my chest

The fear of facing reality is constant

So I keep my eyes closed

I keep silent in this great absurdity

Like a worm

Your eyes despise me

I live crawling in the mud of your indifference

I am something worthless in your life

Deprived of your attention

Denied your respect

Renegade, humiliated, thrown away in the trash

Heartbroken I burst into tears to be heard

But your ears remain deaf

Then with a torn chest I surrender to the dust of your feet

But you shake off the dust and toss me away

The situation in which I find myself is so serious that many laugh at me

I turned into mockery and mockery

From man I became the dirty part of your shoe

The filth of sewage

The impurities of the gutter

An insect that everyone wants to crush

Come and step on my neck

Throw me into the deepest pit of your indignation

And like a worm throws me as far as possible from your love

habit of loving you

I wake up early thinking of you

We make love from the early hours of the day until dusk

A fire consumes us and this hunger to surrender never ends

We are addicted to each other and that will only increases more and more

They accuse us of being sick

Condemn us for all this pleasure

We are a bad example

We always think about giving ourselves

But what does criticism matter?

What good are offenses if we are happy?

Unhappy are those who live lonely

Who spend their days confined in their rooms

Who are distracted by false laughter

Hanging out with fake friends

Trusting your enemies

Pretending a false joy when they cry inside

I love you night and day

I love you non-stop

I have a habit of loving you

Our Love Game

It seems like an endless game

You hurt me and go away

After a while ask for forgiveness and come back to me

We always live like this

Fighting and then forgiving our mistakes

I admit to being a tremendous idiocy

An absurd without this size

We stress, we fight, we hurt

Then we hugged each other, we found everything funny

We exchange confidences, admit our exaggerations

There are times when we cry with laughter

We mock our shortcomings, our failures

We are critical of each other

She thinks I'm crazy and I call her a bitch

In that we live night and day in this stubbornness

In this dull game that turns our coexistence into irony

So much madness was what brought us together, because we are very similar

Who observes us strangely our way of being

But we are completely satisfied in our game of love

Considerations

    Poetry is the most perfect and complete expression of the human spirit, the very definition of love and life reflected through the thought of the poet who transforms in verses and rhymes the joy or pain of the soul that is happy or suffers in silence from words contained deep within your being. This work was written in order to lead our readers to express their most intimate feelings when reading each topic covered and, if they wish, convey to someone as the most perfect outburst.

Lightning Source UK Ltd.
Milton Keynes UK
UKRC011126120720
366357UK00015B/92